WHAT·DO·WE·KNOW ABOUTTHE INUIT·?

BRYAN AND CHERRY ALEXANDER

MACDONALD YOUNG BOOKS

First published in 1995 by
Macdonald Young Books

© 1995 Macdonald Young Books an imprint
of Wayland Publishers Limited

Reprinted in 1996 and 1998 by
Macdonald Young Books
an imprint of Wayland Publishers Limited
61 Western Road
Hove
East Sussex
BN3 1JD

Find Macdonald Young Books on the internet at
http://www.myb.co.uk

Designer and illustrator: Celia Hart
Commissioning editor: Debbie Fox
Copy editor: Jane Booth
Picture research: Val Mulcahy
Series designer: David West

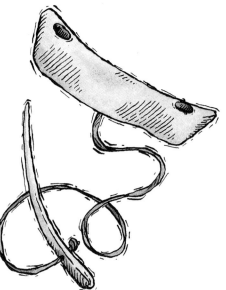

Photograph acknowledgements: Front and back cover: Bryan and Cherry
Alexander; Robert Harding Picture Library, pp9(t), 36(t); Scott Polar Research
Institute, p9(b); Tony Stone Images p43(c)(Daniel J. Cox); Valen Photos,
endpapers (Fred Breumer), p33(r) (John Eastcott/YVA Momatiuk).
All other photographs by Bryan and Cherry Alexander.

Printed in Hong Kong by
Wing King Tong Co. Ltd

A CIP catalogue record for this book
is available from the British Library

ISBN: 0 7500 1728 7 (HB)
      0 7500 2350 3 (PB)

Endpapers: Inuit embroidery and appliqué
work from St Jude's Anglican Cathedral,
Iqaluit. It shows Inuit families with dogsleds
and igloos.

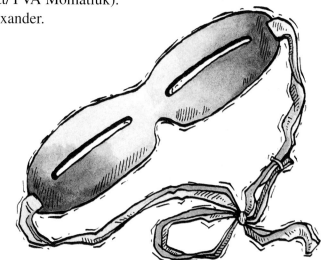

· CONTENTS ·

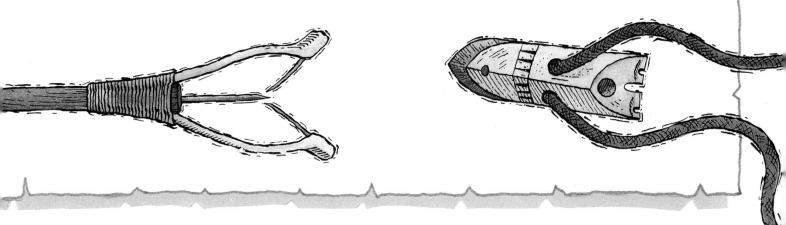

WHO·ARE·THE·INUIT?

The ancestors of the Inuit arrived in the Arctic from Asia crossing the Bering Land Bridge into North America. Later groups would have had to use boats. Today there are about 100,000 Inuit living in the Arctic areas of Siberia, Alaska, Canada and Greenland. They can be divided into two main language groups: the Yupik, who live in Siberia and western Alaska; and the Inupiaq who live in eastern Alaska, Canada and Greenland. Until the arrival of the early explorers in the sixteenth century the world to the south had little impact on the Inuit.

KEY

▨ areas where the Inuit live

▢ extent of summer sea ice

permafrost
⋯⋯ tree line

SIBERIA

North Pole

BERING STRAITS

GREENLAND
Qaanaaq
Savissivik

Barrow

PACIFIC OCEAN

Prudhoe Bay

ALASKA

Igloolik

BAFFIN ISLAND

Holman Island

Iqaluit

INUIT LANDS

The Inuit live in some of the most inhospitable lands in the world. For most of the year the seas are frozen and the land is covered in snow. If you look at the map you will see that most of the Inuit live not far from the coast. Their ancestors made their way from Asia to the east coast of Greenland, probably following the animals they hunted.

YUKON TERRITORY

Arctic Circle

NORTHWEST TERRITORIES

Cape Dorset
Coral Harbour

ATLANTIC OCEAN

Povungnituk

HUDSON BAY

NEWFOUNDLAND

BRITISH COLUMBIA

C A N A D A MANITOBA

QUEBEC

ALBERTA

ONTARIO

SASKATCHEWAN

U S A

HUNTER WITH DOGSLED

This may look like an old photograph but Tatigak looks like this today. He still hunts with his dog team and wears fur clothing in winter. The Inuit are not very tall. Being short helps them to save their body heat when it gets really cold. Their hands, feet and noses are also small so there is less surface area to lose heat from.

POLAR LANDSCAPE

Some say that the Arctic is the area north of the Arctic Circle on the globe (see the map). Others think a better guide is to say it is the area where the ground 1 metre down never thaws. This is called permafrost and it is marked by the tree line. Above you can see the typical polar landscape.

POLAR EXPLORATION

Erik the Red, a Viking, was probably the first explorer to contact the Inuit when he founded a colony in Greenland in AD 983. This print shows the first contact between the Inuit of north-west Greenland and white people, the British naval officers Ross and Parry in 1818. They were looking for the North-West Passage, a shortcut from Europe to the Pacific. Another explorer, John Franklin, died trying to find the route, and many of the men who survived owed their lives to the Inuit who helped them.

 INUIT OR ESKIMO?

The Viking settlers in Greenland called their Inuit neighbours Skraelingar. The name Eskimos was given to them by the Algonquin Indians. It means 'eater of raw meat' because they eat a lot of their food uncooked. The word Inuit means 'people' or 'human beings' and is the name the Inuit give themselves. The word for one person is Inuk. In 1977, the Inuit Circumpolar Conference meeting in Barrow, Alaska, decided that the word Inuit should be used for any Eskimo group whatever they call themselves locally.

TIMELINE

	8000BC	3000–1000BC	1000BC–AD1000	1000–1600	1600–1889	1890–1910
EVENTS IN THE ARCTIC	A group of ancestral Aleuts cross the Bering Land Bridge. Some settle in Alaska, others move to the interior and adapt to tundra hunting.	The group in the interior develop the 'small tool tradition' and move east from Alaska to occupy Canada and Greenland. These are ancestral Inuit.	Alaskan Inuit develop ways of hunting marine mammals and go back into Siberia and across Arctic Canada to Greenland. These people are the Dorset culture and they push out or take over the small tool culture.	During this mild ice-free period, the ancestors of today's Inuit colonise the lands rapidly. They are called the Thule people and are thought to have followed the bowhead whales along the north of Canada to Greenland.	1611 Henry Hudson discovers Hudson Bay. 1721 Pastor Hans Egede colonises Greenland. 1870s Whalers reduce numbers of whales and walrus so much that the Alaskans nearly starve.	1902 Sallirmiut group of Southampton Island is wiped out by a virus. 1903–1906 Amundsen discovers the North-West Passage. 1891–1910 Peary makes repeated attempts on the North Pole and announces success in 1909.
EVENTS IN NORTH AMERICA	17000–7000 Asia and North America are joined by the Bering Land Bridge.			1000 Leif Erikson discovers America.		1898 Engine-driven submarine is invented.

Woolly mammoth

Submarine

	8000BC	3000–1000BC	1000BC–AD1000	1000–1600	1600–1889	1890–1910
EVENTS IN EUROPE		1700 Start of Bronze Age in Western Europe.	AD983 Erik the Red discovers Greenland. AD1066 Normans invade Britain at Hastings.	1347–91 Black Death sweeps across Europe killing up to a half of the population.	1789 French Revolution. 1859 Charles Darwin writes *Origin of Species*. 1866 Swedish scientist Nobel invents dynamite.	1897 Diamond Jubilee of Queen Victoria.

Deathmask of Tutankhamun

Queen Victoria

	8000BC	3000–1000BC	1000BC–AD1000	1000–1600	1600–1889	1890–1910
EVENTS AROUND THE WORLD	4000 Potter's wheel is invented in Mesopotamia. 3760 First year of Jewish calendar.	1352 Death of King Tutankhamun in Egypt.	300BC Height of Maya civilisation in Central and South America. 236BC Building of Great Wall of China is begun.	1000 Gunpowder is invented in China. 1272 Marco Polo visits China. 1492 Christopher Columbus discovers America.	1787 Botany Bay in Australia is chosen as a colony for convicts.	

Great Wall of China

1911–1950	1951–1979	1980–1989	1990–1999
1921–24 Knud Rasmussen travels across Arctic America to visit and document nearly all the Inuit groups.	1953 116 Inuit are moved by the government to make way for Thule Air Base. 1972 First native self-government is set up in Barrow, Alaska. 1979 Greenland receives home rule from Denmark.	1981 Greenland votes to leave the European Community. 1982 European Community bans the import of seal products and hampers development of Inuit economy.	1993 Nunavut is confirmed. 1999 Nunavut comes into force.
1942 Nuclear chain reaction is discovered.	**Buddy Holly** 1959 Rock-and-Roll star Buddy Holly is killed in a plane crash.		1992 Bill Clinton elected President of the USA.
1928 Alexander Fleming discovers penicillin. 1925 John Logie Baird invents TV. **Television**	1961 Berlin Wall is built to divide Communist East Berlin from West Berlin.	1986 First triple organ transplant of heart, lungs and liver in Cambridge, UK.	1991 Hostilities break out in Yugoslavia.
1948 South African government introduces policy of apartheid – separating the lives of black and white citizens.	1957–75 Vietnam war. 1974 Terracotta army is discovered buried near Xian, China.		1991 Gulf war. 1991 Communist rule ends in the USSR.

THE THULE CULTURE

The Thule culture people are believed to be the ancestors of today's Inuit. This culture is named after Thule in north-west Greenland because that is where the first remains were found. It is thought that the people came from north Alaska around AD1000 and that they quickly colonised the whole of Arctic Canada. At this time it was warmer than it is today and they could have been following the bowhead whales through the northern sea ways. There are large amounts of whalebone around the remains of early Thule culture camps and they could have killed enough whales in the summer months to provide food right through the winter months. Around 1200 the climate started to cool. It is suspected that many Thule villagers died, and those who did survive had to learn skills to help them live in the harsher climate.

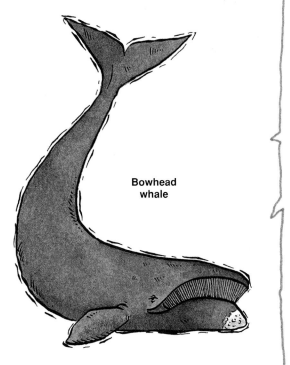

Bowhead whale

DOGSLEDS

There is evidence that some of the pre-Dorset cultures used dogs to help with their hunting. The first evidence of the use of the dogsleds was found in Thule culture sites where bones drilled to make sled runners and dog whip handles have been found.

WHERE·DO THE·INUIT GET.THEIR ·FOOD?·

Because it is very cold in the far north where the Inuit live, they cannot grow any crops and rely on the meat of animals they can hunt in the sea and on the land around them for food. Most Inuit groups hunt seals, polar bears and walrus. Some groups can also hunt land animals like caribou and musk oxen. Fish can be plentiful, but for much of the year must be caught through holes in the ice with hooks, nets or *kakivaks*. Inuit living in towns can go to the shops and buy food but it is very expensive because it has to be shipped in from the south. They can buy meat from their neighbours who hunt. This is often called 'country food'.

AN INUK SETS HIS SEAL NET
When the sea ice is still thin and new in the autumn, some Inuit set nets under the ice to catch seals. They put the nets where they know the seals will swim, usually where there is a strong current in the water. The Inuit visit these nets regularly to remove any seals they have caught. Seal meat is an important part of the diet of most Inuit groups.

101 USES FOR A DEAD CARIBOU

The caribou was like a department store to the ancestors of today's Inuit. Not only could they eat the meat, but the skin was used to make tents, bedding and clothing. Thread was made from the sinews and needles were made from bones. The antlers were always useful for harpoons and arrowheads or snow goggles.

INUK HUNTER WITH A CARIBOU
An Inuk has just shot a caribou using a high-powered rifle with telescopic sights. He has travelled to the caribou herd by snowscooter. Caribou meat is very high in protein. It has twice as much protein as beef per 100 grams. It is also very low in fat. As long as the Inuit also eat the liver, caribou will provide an almost complete diet, high in vitamin C and lacking only vitamin D, which they can get from fish.

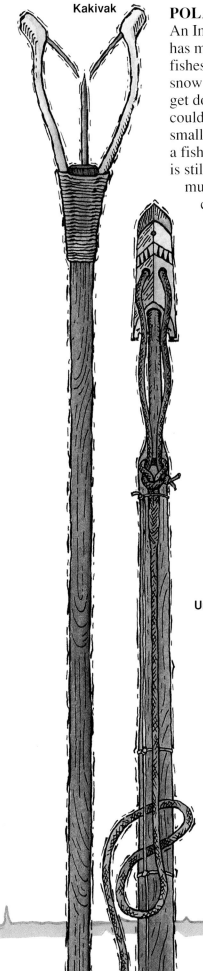

Kakivak

Unaaq

POLAR INUK FISHING

An Inuk sits by a hole he has made in the sea ice and fishes. Look at how much snow he had to dig away to get down to the ice before he could make a hole. He jigs a small lure up and down until a fish grabs it in its mouth. It is still very cold so the Inuk must wear lots of warm clothes.

HUNTING TOOLS

Many Inuit today hunt with rifles, but in the north-west of Greenland the *unaaq* is still used because the local hunting laws say that certain prey must be harpooned before being shot. The *unaaq* has a long rope attached to a float made of an inflated sealskin or a tyre inner tube. The *kakivak* is a three-pronged fish spear used to catch fish through a hole in the ice or in pools in the summer.

FOOD SHOPPING IN THE NORTH

Food shops in every village mean that the Inuit no longer starve when hunting is bad, but these foods are less nutritious than 'country foods', and foods that go off, like dairy produce or fruit, are often very expensive because they are flown up from the south.

DO · THE · INUIT · EAT · WELL ?

Because they have only meat and fish to eat most of the year, the Inuit have a diet which is very high in protein and fats. Medical research has shown this diet to be very healthy for them. Few Inuit have cancer, diabetes or heart disease. They manage without fruit and vegetables because whale skin and seal liver contain as much vitamin C as oranges or grapefruit. In times of plenty the Inuit preserve food for times when hunting is poor. They dry it, bury it and of course, they freeze it. In the brief summer months they gather plants, flowers and berries, and fish in inland lakes.

EATING RAW SEAL LIVER

These girls don't mind getting blood all over their hands as they eat raw, warm seal liver. They always eat it with their fingers. If they are out on a hunting trip with their family it saves time not having to cook a meal. The Inuit eat other foods raw too. *Muktuk* is a chewy layer of gristle found below the skin of a narwhal. It is cut into bite-sized pieces with a sharp knife and then it is eaten with some salt. The Inuit eat *muktuk* raw because they prefer it that way. It is also higher in vitamin C when it is raw so they don't need to eat fresh fruit.

'I would like to say a few words about this land. The only food I like is meat.'

Salluviniq, Resolute Bay.

HANGING FISH UP TO DRY

When the summer arrives the Inuit like to go fishing for Arctic char in lakes that still have a covering of ice. This means they can fish in the deepest waters without having to use a boat. The fish are a very valuable addition to the diet because they contain vitamin D. To dry the fish the Inuit first fillet them, then cut the flesh across in squares so that the dry Arctic air can remove the moisture from the fish meat. When the fish have been hanging for a while they are put into sacks and used throughout the winter months as a change from seal meat or caribou.

CATCHING BIRDS

In spring, the little auks arrive. They are small black and white sea birds that nest in holes under rocks on hillsides by the sea. The Inuit catch them in huge numbers using a long-handled net called an *ipua*. This can be hard because the birds fly very fast. The Inuit eat them raw, cooked, or they put them in a sealskin and bury them for many months until they are rotten, then they are a delicacy called *kaviak*.

DANGEROUS FOODS

There are foods that the Inuit know not to eat. One of these is polar bear liver which is so high in vitamin A that it is poisonous. When a bear is killed the Inuit are careful not to let the huskies eat the liver. Polar bears, walrus and bearded seals sometimes also have parasites and their meat must be cooked to be safe to eat.

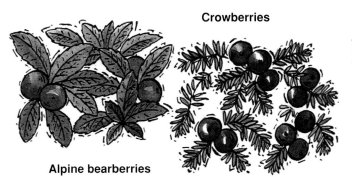

Crowberries

Alpine bearberries

COLLECTING PLANTS AND BERRIES

The short summer gives the Inuit a variety in their diet. They eat the nectar from purple saxifrage, the bark from Arctic willow, the sharp vitamin-rich leaves of sorrel and several kinds of berries.

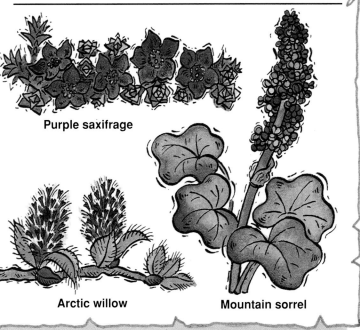

Purple saxifrage

Arctic willow

Mountain sorrel

· HOW · DO · THE · INUIT · SURVIVE · THE · COLD ?

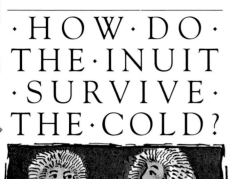

The far north is very cold. In winter it is also dark for a long time. In some areas the sun sets at the end of October and doesn't rise again until early February. Even during the coldest time of year, the Inuit still have to hunt for food. Hunters sometimes may have to travel great distances. At this time much of the sea is frozen. It is a good time to hunt for walrus and polar bears. In summer the sea thaws for a few weeks but it can still have a thin film of ice on it at night in sheltered bays. Despite temperatures as low as -50°C, the Inuit have developed ways of thriving in their ice-bound surroundings.

ICE-FREE SUMMER

In summer, the 24 hours of sunlight boosts life in the sea and migratory birds come from as far away as the Antarctic to feed and breed. The Inuit hunt from *kayaks* when the sea is ice free. They harpoon narwhals using a throwing board which gives leverage to drive the harpoon through the air. The Inuhuit have strict rules which say that in certain areas they must hunt with a harpoon before a whale is shot or lanced to death. They understand that to kill too many animals will mean there will be none for future generations to hunt.

POLAR NIGHT AND MIDNIGHT SUN

The reason that the polar regions have continuous darkness in winter and continuous daylight in summer is because the Earth's axis is tilted at an angle to the sun as it spins around it.

As you can see from the illustration, in June the North Pole is towards the sun, and at this time the sun can always be seen in the sky, in December the opposite is true.

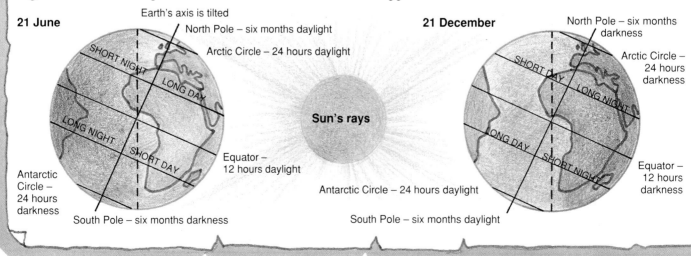

21 June
Earth's axis is tilted
North Pole – six months daylight
Arctic Circle – 24 hours daylight
SHORT NIGHT
LONG DAY
LONG NIGHT
SHORT DAY
Equator – 12 hours daylight
Antarctic Circle – 24 hours darkness
South Pole – six months darkness

Sun's rays

21 December
North Pole – six months darkness
Arctic Circle – 24 hours darkness
SHORT DAY
LONG NIGHT
LONG DAY
SHORT NIGHT
Equator – 12 hours darkness
Antarctic Circle – 24 hours daylight
South Pole – six months daylight

INUIT RUNNING TO KEEP WARM

The temperature in the Arctic in the winter can plunge to -50°C, and even wrapped in many layers of fur clothing, it can be cold sitting on a sled. One way the Inuit have of keeping warm is to run behind their sleds until their blood is circulating to their hands and feet and they have warmed up enough to sit down again.

THE SKILL OF KEEPING WARM

The Inuit are experts at keeping warm on the coldest of days. Early Antarctic explorers used to travel north first to buy clothing from the Inuit before setting off to the opposite end of the Earth. Inuit clothes made of caribou fur are so warm because every hair is hollow and traps the air in an insulating layer. Polar bear fur works in a different way. Every transparent hair carries light from the sun down to the black skin of the polar bear, which absorbs the heat.

SNOW COVERED HUSKY

Huskies are tough dogs that the Inuit use to pull their sleds across winter snow and ice. They have thick coats and when it gets cold they curl up into tight balls and wrap their fluffy tails over their feet and noses to keep them warm. In this way they can sleep soundly through the worst Arctic storms, insulated under a blanket of snow.

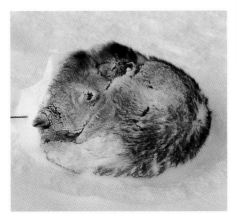

PUTTING BOOTS ON HUSKIES

When the sea ice starts to thaw in the summer it forms sharp needles of ice on its surface that can cut the paws of huskies, which are already softened by running on the wet ice. To prevent serious injury the Inuit make boots for the dogs from bits of oilskin or canvas with holes cut for the front claws. This enables the huskies to grip when pulling the sled.

DO·THE INUIT·HAVE ·FAMILIES· LIKE·OURS?

MOTHER WITH CHILD

An Inuit mother carries her baby in an *amaut* on her back. The child takes warmth from its mother's body – a pram would be much too cold. Moss would have been used to keep the baby dry, but now mothers use disposable nappies.

Most Inuit families are similar to our own with mother, father and children living in one house. Sometimes an older relative may live with the family and their experience and skills in sewing or making hunting implements is a valuable contribution to the household. A young hunter will marry as soon as he can support a wife because he needs someone to clean his skins and make fur clothes for him. Nowadays many Inuit girls would rather marry young men with jobs in a town as they will have money, and being a hunter's wife is very hard work. Children are carried by their mothers in an *amaut* for the first year, but as soon as they are walking everyone takes a turn in looking after them. Grandparents often live close by and like to help.

EXTENDED HUNTING FAMILY

Up to sixteen people live at this outpost camp in this hunting hut on Baffin Island where there is often good caribou hunting during the winter. While the men go out and hunt, the women clean skins and do other chores and everybody shares the meat and the hard work. The children learn about life by watching members of their extended family.

ITUKU AND PANERAK AT HOME

Ituku holds his son Igayak while his wife Panerak softens a piece of sealskin by chewing it. They live together in this one-roomed house which was built by Ituku's father. Inuit children grow up seeing their parents feeding dogs and working with skins. These will be vital skills if they are to follow their parents into a life of hunting. But no one will put pressure on them to learn until they are ready to do so.

AN ELDERLY INUK WITH HIS GRANDSON

This man and his grandson spend as much time together as they can. The Inuit believe that the family is very important. Grandparents will often adopt a grandchild if there is any problem with his parents keeping him or her. This boy lives with his parents but he loves to be with his best friend, his grandfather.

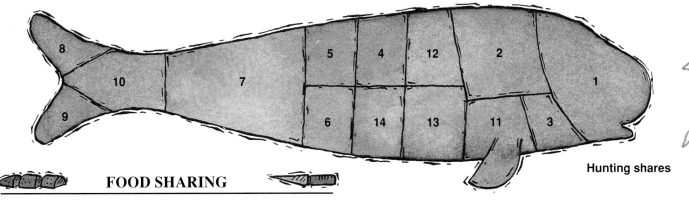

Hunting shares

FOOD SHARING

In the past the Inuit always lived with the threat of starvation. If the hunting failed it was not uncommon for old people to be left behind to starve. Parents would even kill their own babies rather than watch them starve when there was no more breast milk. To avoid this awful fate there has always been a system of food sharing. Good hunters have always shared their meat with the less skilled in their family. Men out hunting together always share the animal that they have killed. In this way, families from a whole village can benefit from several men going on a walrus hunt. The huge amount of meat needed to feed a team of huskies makes sure no one gets lazy.

HUNTING SHARES

This diagram of a whale shows how it would be divided among hunters. The harpooner gets parts 1, 2, 3 and 10 as well as the heart and intestines. If there is a second harpooner he is entitled to sections 7, 8 and 9. Others who have helped with lancing or towing the whale to shore are entitled to a share from the parts numbered 4, 5, 6, 11, 12, 13 and 14. Other animals that are hunted are also divided into shares. Very little of an animal is wasted.

D O · T H E · I N U I T · L I V E · I N H O U S E S ?

The Inuit word for house is *iglu*. What we call an igloo is an *igluigaq* or snowhouse to them. In the past, only a few of the Inuit groups lived in igloos in the winter months and most lived in turf houses built from local materials, which were small and easy to keep warm. The Inuit lived in scattered groups close to hunting grounds, moving on from time to time. Governments in the Arctic now prefer the Inuit to live in communities as these are easier to administer. These towns are often not in good places for hunting so hunters have to travel long distances to hunt or rely on welfare payments from the government to live.

IGLOOS

There were many different types of snowhouses ranging from simple temporary shelters to complex many-domed living quarters. The snow blocks used in an *igluigaq* are cut either with a large knife or a saw. These blocks are built round in a spiral, with the top blocks leaning in to form a dome. The joints are made to fit by shaving off snow between blocks with the snow knife. The final block in the top of the roof is put in with great care. In many areas in Canada, children take igloo building as a lesson in school.

INSIDE AN IGLOO

This Inuk from Greenland uses an igloo as an overnight shelter. He will light a Primus stove to cook on and to warm the igloo.

IGLOO AT NIGHT

Light shines out from between the snow blocks of an igloo during a long polar night. The igloo is shelter from the wind and air trapped in the snow insulates it.

AN INUIT VILLAGE – SAVISSIVIK

Today many Inuit live in villages in houses made of timber shipped up from the south. They are larger, harder to heat and have separate bedrooms which is unusual for an Inuit house. Stilts are used to keep them off the permafrost.

TURF HOUSE

Like the igloo, the design of the turf house varied throughout the Arctic, and was influenced by the materials available. In Alaska there was always wood and whalebone as a support for the turf, but in other areas they used only turf and rocks. Mostly the houses consisted of a low wall of stone or turf with roofs made from whatever was available. The entrance was a sunken tunnel that helped to keep the warm air in the house. Because they were easy and inexpensive to build, a family could have a house in each of their hunting areas.

Turf house

INSIDE A MODERN HOUSE

This modern house in Savissivik has electricity from a generator to run the TV and hi-fi. It is warm enough to sit in a t-shirt and most of all it has space to stand up and walk around. These luxuries show this family has a good cash income.

WHAT·DO THE·INUIT ·WEAR?·

It is very cold in the Arctic, but the Inuit know how to dress for the snow and the biting winds. They have learnt how to use the insulating properties of the skins of the animals they eat to make warm clothes. Until white people came the Inuit had no woven fabrics. Even though they can now buy woollen clothes in the shop they still prefer to wear skins when they are out on the land because nothing else keeps them as warm. The furs they use will depend on the animals they can hunt.

SOFTENING SKIN BY CHEWING

Sealskin is used to make boots called *kamik*. The dried skin is cut out into shapes and then softened by chewing it along folds. The front teeth are used so the skin doesn't get too soggy. The teeth of lots of older women are worn right down from doing this over many years. Dentists have told them to hammer the skin instead of chewing it, but this damages the fibres of the skin and it is not properly waterproof. So everyone still chews skins.

Sealskin mittens

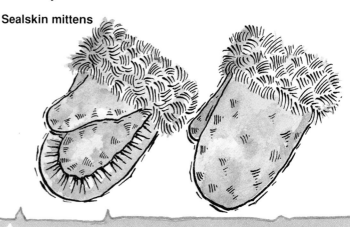

INUK DRESSED IN FURS

The Inuhuit have a lot of polar bears in their area, so Kigutikak is wearing *nannuk* – polar bear skin trousers. He is also wearing a caribou skin parka, a *qulittaq*, which has a blue fox trim on the hood. His sealskin boots, *kamik*, have soles of bearded sealskin and an inner sock of sheepskin or the fur of Arctic hares.

MODERN DRESS

These little girls are playing on toboggans outside the school building. Parents prefer to dress their children in clothes and boots bought from stores. If they get cold they can always go inside to warm up. Clothes made from man-made fabrics like these are easy to keep clean and much less trouble to maintain than furs, and are the choice of everyone but the oldest in the village. But if the Inuit go out on the land during the winter they will probably wear furs.

TRADITIONAL THERMAL UNDERWEAR

Today the Inuit can go into the store and buy thermal underwear to go under their very warm fur clothes. Before there was a shop they used natural materials, making vests out of the skin of sea birds, worn with the feathers on the inside, and socks from the skins of Arctic hares. These all tore very easily and couldn't be washed.

DRYING SKIN

All skins must be cleaned before they are stretched on a wooden frame to dry. Some of the sealskins will have the fur left on them to make clothing, but others will be used for making *kamik* and will have the fur removed.

Drying frame

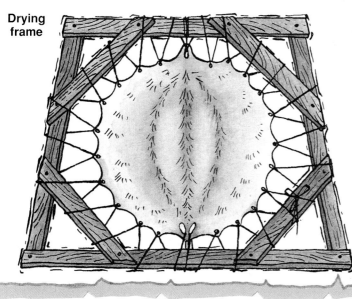

WOMAN MAKING BOOTS

Although these traditional *kamik* are made of sealskin they are not being sewn with *ivaluq*, which is a thread made from dried narwhal sinews. Everyone now uses dental floss instead.

DO · THE · INUIT · GO · TO · WORK?

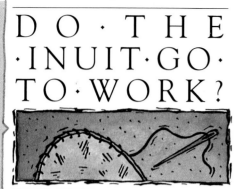

Hunting for enough meat to feed their families and the huskies, as well as maintaining hunting equipment is hard work. Women clean skins and also often fetch the ice that will be melted for all the water the family uses. The Inuit are not paid for any of these tasks. In the past they found everything they needed on the land, but now they need cash to pay for goods such as fuel, bullets, toilet paper, coffee and sugar. Life is easier for an Inuk with a job as he earns cash. The Inuit used to sell seal and fox skins for the money they needed, but now there is no market for those furs and many families have been badly affected.

INUK FEEDING DOGS

Traditionally dogsleds have been essential to the Inuit. A hunter will use between two and fifteen huskies, but he needs to be a good hunter to feed a large team of dogs. A man will need to feed more meat to his dog team than to his wife and children. During the winter the team is fed every other day. A meal of chunks of raw walrus meat takes a long time to digest and provides the energy needed for long journeys. During the summer when they are not working the dogs are fed less often.

Ulus

WORK OR PLAY?

The Inuit who live traditionally don't divide their day into work and leisure time. A lot of effort is needed just to keep everyone fed and clothed. It is not possible to work a nine-to-five day in the Arctic because the weather influences everything. The Inuhuit say, 'The wind carries sleep', because in bad weather everyone dozes indoors until it is over. But in the summer when the weather is fine and the sun doesn't set, everyone keeps too busy to get a lot of sleep.

WOMAN CARRYING ICE
Icebergs are the main source of water for some Inuit groups and often the icebergs are a long way from the village. Just collecting ice can take up a lot of time. Care must be taken not to collect any sea ice by mistake as this is too salty.

CLEANING A SKIN
Panerak uses a woman's knife, called an ulu (left), to scrape the fat off a sealskin. She takes great care not to make any holes in the skin. She will also use the ulu for cutting meat. Her husband is a great hunter and she always has need of a sharp knife.

WORKING IN A SHOP
In each of the small villages there are only one or two shops. This young man is moving soft drinks from the store room to the shop. He is one of the few Inuit who earns cash but he may still choose to hunt at weekends.

WHAT·DO THE·INUIT DO·IN·THEIR SPARE·TIME?

The Inuit spend most of their time hunting for food, making clothes and keeping their homes warm. Their lives are not divided into work and leisure, but they do have things that they enjoy doing. Everyone enjoys visiting their neighbours, and these social visits strengthen the community spirit within the village. In times of bad weather or during the Polar Night (see page 16) the Inuit families like telling stories about exciting hunts or the silly things people have done. The Inuit like to laugh a lot. Children have plenty of spare time during which they learn skills by copying the adults around them. Traditionally the Inuit only played a skin drum, but with the introduction of other instruments they have found they enjoy music.

STRING PUZZLES

Mikisuk makes an *ajarraaq*, or string puzzle, of a tent. This is one of the easiest puzzles to do. Some puzzles are very complicated and have stories or rhymes to go with them. They all use a simple loop of string like a cat's cradle, but the Inuit would once have used a thin thong of sealskin. Mikisuk was taught dozens of string games by her grandmother. Many cultures all over the world have a tradition of string puzzles.

GOING VISITING WITH A TEACUP

Saufak always carries her own teacup when she makes a visit because the person she is visiting may not have a spare cup for her, especially if several people are already there. In the 1940s, when there was a risk of catching tuberculosis, everyone was told to use their own cup. The Inuit still follow this advice today, which is important as the disease is present in the Arctic again. Visiting plays an important part in keeping the ties of the family and village strong.

PLAYING ON THE ICE

These children are playing on sea ice that has been broken by the action of the tide. It is a dangerous game. There is always the risk that if they fall into the water they will be swept under the broken ice and drown. The sea water is close to or below 0°C. In this harsh environment, Inuit children need to learn how to cope with the different types of ice while they are still young.

GAMES AND PASTIMES

The Inuit play lots of games that test certain skills. The *ajagaq* is a ring and pin game and needs good coordination to toss the large bone and catch it on the bone spike. Wooden handles joined with a sealskin thong are used for tug of war between two people seated on the ground.

Ajagaq

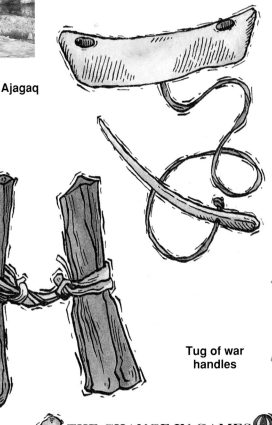

Tug of war handles

GIRL PLAYING A GUITAR

Some Inuit children like to learn to play musical instruments. Traditional Inuit music uses only a drum, but a guitar is more in keeping with popular music. Now they can play the songs of an Inuhuit band called 'Flying Kayak' which is a popular group in Greenland.

THE CHANGE IN GAMES

The Inuit have always been very good at using things that are close at hand, and making their games from scraps. In the past they made balls from the bladder of a seal, which they blew up then left to dry. They also played a game similar to 'jacks' which was made from bones from a seal flipper. Inuit children today buy frisbees and plastic footballs at the shop.

·DO·BOYS· AND·GIRLS ·GO·TO· SCHOOL?

The school is a very important part of any Inuit village. Before schools were introduced, the children used to travel with their parents as they moved from camp to camp. When the Canadian government wanted to encourage the Inuit to move into villages, they offered them housing and medical facilities. It was only when the children were forced to attend school that their parents finally moved into the villages to be near them. The children learnt from books about life in the south and in doing so missed out on learning the traditional Inuit skills from their parents.

THE CLASSROOM
The children sit on the floor around the feet of their teacher in this school in Coral Harbour, in Canada's North-West Territories. Their teacher is an Inuit woman and she is showing them pictures in a book. She is a good example to them because she shows them that it is possible to be an Inuit and have a good job, like being a teacher. Teachers in the Canadian Arctic earn a good wage. For many years all children could expect after ten years' schooling was a low-paid job.

GIRLS USING A COMPUTER
Schools in the Canadian north are well equipped. Computers programmed for both syllabics (see opposite) and our alphabet mean Inuit pupils like the girls in this photograph can work in their own language. They also have excellent indoor sport facilities.

Education is now even more important because to be successful Nunavut (see page 42) will need educated Inuktitut speakers. As well as computing, girls are taught traditional skills like beadwork at school.

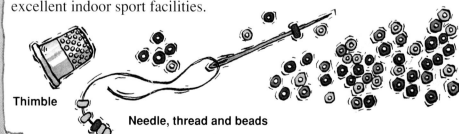

Thimble

Needle, thread and beads

MAKING A SLED
In the school in Savissivik the boys learn to make a traditional wooden sled. Nothing is nailed and to keep it flexible everything is joined with lashings. The girls have lessons in sewing sealskins.

HUNTING WITH FATHER
The day an Inuit boy kills his first seal is considered very important. He learns the necessary skills from his father. When hunting *utoq*, or sleeping seal, he stalks it using a white cotton screen about 1 metre square. He approaches slowly and quietly until he is close enough to get a good shot.

LANGUAGE AND SYLLABICS
When schools were first introduced into the Arctic the lessons were not in the native language. In Canada the lessons were taught in English by white teachers, most of whom could not speak Inuktitut. The children could not understand them. Today there are Inuit teachers in most communities. It is now understood that the language and the culture are closely linked, and schools have been putting more emphasis on Inuktitut. Inuktitut is written in syllabics, a set of shapes that represent sounds (see below). Using the triangles in slightly different positions can change the meaning of a word totally.

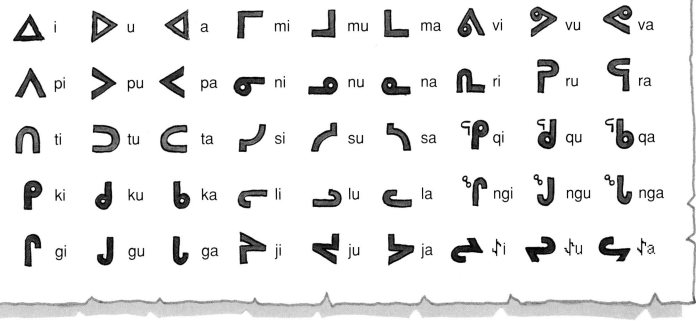

△ i	▷ u	◁ a	Γ mi	⌐ mu	L ma	⋏ vi	⋗ vu	⋖ va
⋀ pi	⋗ pu	⋖ pa	⌐ ni	⌐ nu	⌐ na	⋔ ri	⊐ ru	⊏ ra
⋂ ti	⊐ tu	⊏ ta	⌐ si	⌐ su	⌐ sa	⋔ qi	⊐ qu	⊏ qa
P ki	⋔ ku	⊏ ka	⌐ li	⊐ lu	⊏ la	⋔ ngi	⊐ ngu	⊏ nga
Γ gi	J gu	⊏ ga	⊿ ji	⋏ ju	⋗ ja	⊿ ᵗi	⋏ ᵗu	⋖ ᵗa

ARE·THE ·INUIT· ARTISTS?

The Inuit have always produced beautiful things, but haven't thought of them as being art. No one can be really sure what the tiny figures that are found in archaeological sites were used for. Maybe they were tiny toys for the children or hunting talismans. In more recent times the Inuit have turned their skills to making prints and stone sculptures to sell to collectors in the south. Many are of the birds and animals found in the Arctic and characters from folk tales and hunting stories.

MABEL MAKES A PRINT

Mabel Nigiyak is an Inuit artist from the Holman Island Art Cooperative. She is working on a design that will be made into a stonecut print by her daughter. They will print a limited number of this design. This form of art is popular with collectors in the south and a catalogue is published every year so buyers will know what is available.

PITSEOLAK

Pitseolak was a very famous Inuit artist from Cape Dorset on Baffin Island. She was already very old when she was asked why she painted. She replied, 'Firstly I did it for the money, but now I hope that when I die I can continue to paint in Heaven.'

INUK CARVES IN STONE
Nukapianguak is carving a fur-clad hunter with his raised arm holding a harpoon. This is made from a very hard local north Greenlandic stone. Usually carvings are made from soapstone because it is much softer and easier to work with.

Decorated hunting parka

DECORATED FUR PARKAS
The Copper Inuit who live in the western Arctic use an ornate border to decorate the hems of their hunting parkas. It is called 'delta trim' and is made by sewing light- and dark-haired pieces of caribou skin in a geometric design. It takes about a month to make enough trim like this for the bottom of a parka.

THE LEGEND CARVINGS
In 1958, the Reverend Steinmann encouraged his parishioners in Povungnituk to try carving their local legends in soapstone. This was the first attempt to use sculpture as a way of earning money. This soapstone is of an Inuk wrestling with a *tuniq*.

31

· D O · T H E · INUIT · WRITE · B O O K S ? ·

The Inuit have no tradition of writing and all their history was passed on by word of mouth until the missionaries arrived in each region. In Canada, the missionaries devised a system of recording words called syllabics using shapes that describe the sounds. In Greenland they used the same alphabet we do, which was much easier. Many of the world's great works of literature have been translated into Greenlandic, but few into syllabics. The Inuit had a rich oral tradition which has been written down by many explorers and ethnographers. Now the Inuit read comics, books and newspapers like the *Nunatsiaq News*.

RECORDING STORIES

Noah is an elderly Iglulingmiut and he is taking part in a community project to document the lives of the village elders. Many elderly Inuit are now recording stories about their younger days before they settled in the villages. In this way the information won't be lost when they die. They talk about ghosts visiting hunters' huts and about hunters performing great feats of strength. Stories that have been handed down the generations and explain the origins of things like the sun and the moon are called myths.

A TRADITIONAL STORY

In the olden days, all birds were white. And then one day the Raven and the Loon fell to drawing patterns on each other's feathers. The Raven began, and when it had finished, the Loon was so displeased with the pattern that it spat all over the Raven and made it black all over. And since that day all ravens have been black. But the Raven was so angry that it fell upon the Loon and beat it so about the legs that it could hardly walk. And that is why the loon is such an awkward creature on land.

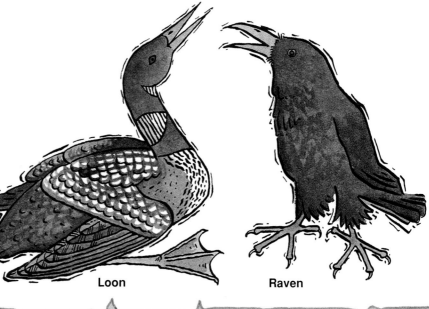

Loon   Raven

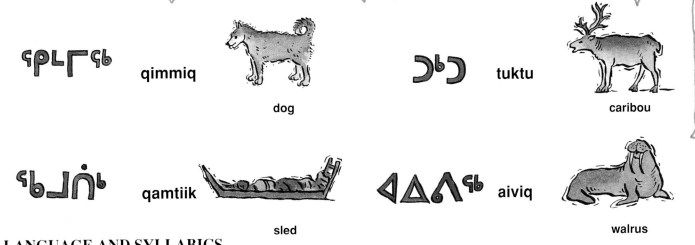

ᖅᒻᒥᖅ **qimmiq**
dog

ᖃᒧᑏᒃ **qamtiik**
sled

ᑐᒃᑐ **tuktu**
caribou

ᐊᐃᕕᖅ **aiviq**
walrus

ᓇᓄᖅ **nanuq**
polar bear

LANGUAGE AND SYLLABICS

Above are some common Inuktitut words in our alphabet and syllabics. Below is a warning sign on a building in Canada. By law it must be written in English and French. But some of the Inuit don't speak either of those languages, so an additional warning has been added in syllabics.

THE CREATION STORY

You can tell how well the oral tradition has worked because Inuit communities separated by thousands of miles share myths and stories which are virtually identical. For example, the myth of 'the woman who married a dog' is known in similar forms from Siberia to Greenland. In this story the woman becomes Sedna, the important spirit of the sea, who has control over all sea mammals. In some versions her children become Indians and white people, in another her cut-off fingers become the animals of the sea. Another myth found in almost all groups is that of 'Brother Moon and Sister Sun'. This is a story of disappointed lovers, a brother and sister, who both carry flaming torches as he pursues her across the night sky. They also have myths of great floods like the Noah's Ark story in the Bible.

READING A COMIC

This little girl is sitting on the floor reading a comic. Her mother and father would have sat around a seal oil lamp and listened to the older people telling stories and talking about hunting, but now the art of storytelling is dying.

· DO · THE · INUIT · GO · TO · THE · DOCTOR ? ·

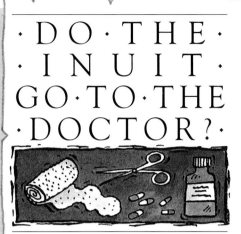

Most villages in the Arctic are small and only a few have a permanent doctor. Doctors make regular visits to villages and hunting camps to give routine care, such as vaccinations and general check-ups. If anyone is seriously ill they will be flown to one of the hospitals in a big town, but mostly they will be given medicine by the nurse in the village. In the north of Greenland the dentist only visits twice a year. He travels between villages by dogsled and sets up his surgery in the church, which is often also the school. An optician also visits once a year to check everyone's eyesight.

DOCTOR VISITING AN INUIT FAMILY

This doctor is visiting Tabitha and her family at a hunting camp near their home village of Siorapaluk. He will check their health and give the baby any vaccinations that are due. The nearest hospital is in the town of Qaanaaq which is one day away by dogsled or boat in case of emergencies.

 ## CAUGHT IN THE MIDDLE

When government administrators encouraged the Inuit to settle in villages they thought it would be safer and better for them. But by changing the lifestyle of the Inuit groups, new problems were introduced. What the government didn't realise was how the Inuit would suffer because they found it hard to adapt from being independent nomadic hunters to living in villages where they are dependent on having money. Suicides, crimes related to alcohol and more recently drug abuse have reached most of the large settlements.

NUMBERED BOTTLES

In northern Greenland each village has a nurse. If someone is ill she can consult with a doctor by radio. She describes the symptoms and the doctor tells her which medicines to use. These are kept in numbered bottles.

Medicines

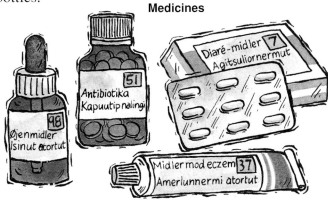

THE WHALERS BROUGHT DISEASES

After 1850, the Inuit were regularly visited by whalers as they came north each year for the whales. Sometimes the crews carried with them killer diseases such as smallpox, tuberculosis, measles and influenza, to which the Inuit had no immunity. In some areas as many as half the people in a community died.

A DENTIST ARRIVES BY HELICOPTER

A dentist is watching the unloading of all his boxes at the village of Moriussaq in north Greenland (above). Helicopters are faster than dogsleds and they are used a great deal in Greenland where the land is often too mountainous to have runways for fixed-wing planes. In Canada they use fixed-wing planes throughout the Arctic and when there is a medical emergency the pilots will brave the worst of weathers to save a life. Medical help by air wasn't introduced until the early 1950s.

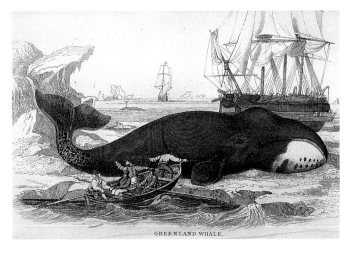

GREENLAND WHALE.

·DO·THE· ·INUIT· BELIEVE·IN LIFE· AFTER ·DEATH?·

The Inuit believe that the spirit of a person who has recently died will divide into two. The personal soul goes to a place where there is always warmth and plenty of animals to hunt, while the soul of the name of the person remains on Earth until a new baby is given that name, and with it their skills and personality. Today most Inuit are Christians, but some older Inuit can still remember when everyone believed they could influence their lives by communicating with spirits. They had rules or 'taboos' for all aspects of their lives and if they kept to these they believed their lives would go smoothly. The person who helped them to communicate with these spirits was an *angakkuq* or shaman.

CHRISTIANITY

The first missionary in the north was the Norwegian priest Hans Egede in 1745, but soon after that there were missionaries working in the eastern Arctic and Alaska. These priests thought the complex superstitions that the Inuit believed in were pagan and they wanted the Inuit to accept Christianity instead. They began to change the beliefs of the Inuit by destroying the system of taboos and the leadership of the shamans. In east Greenland the shamans were among the first to convert to Christianity. Without the guidance of the taboos, the Inuit culture started to collapse.

GRAVES ON THE TUNDRA

It is very hard to bury anything in tundra because as the ground thaws and refreezes each year the largest objects come to the surface, just like when you shake a bag of mixed stones the largest rise to the top. In this way the bones in a grave finally come to the top. They are always treated with great respect. Before the arrival of the missionaries the Inuhuit would sew a dead body into a skin, carry it some distance, then place it on the ground facing the rising sun. The body was then buried under rocks along with the person's belongings.

DRUMSINGING

Drumsinging is common to all Inuit groups. It was used by the shaman for special ceremonies and for entertainment. Singing and dancing usually went with drumming. Drumsinging was even used to settle disputes, as the best drummer was judged to be right.

 ## TABOOS

Taboos are things the Inuit did to keep the great spirits happy. Powerful spirits such as Sedna who had control over all the animals that lived in the sea, as well as storms and foul weather, was treated with respect. As all animals were thought to have souls, when they were killed they would be offered gifts of food and water. By offering this kindness the Inuit believed the animals would allow themselves to be killed again in the future. Another taboo involved cutting a hole in the wall of the igloo when a person died as it was forbidden to take a body out of the house through the door. The Inuit believed that to break a taboo would bring bad luck and poor hunting on the family.

TUPILAKS

Tupilaks were used in Greenland for 5,000 years to get rid of enemies. They were carved from ivory in a secret place. These monsters were thought to become real and destroy the victim, unless stronger magic turned them against their maker. Now they are sold to tourists as souvenirs of the Arctic.

Tupilaks

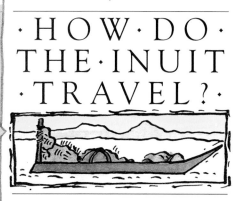

· HOW · DO · THE · INUIT · TRAVEL? ·

In the winter months when the sea is frozen and snow covers the land, the Inuit travel on sleds pulled by a team of huskies. In the summer when the snow melts and the sea ice breaks up, the Inuit travel by boat. Traditionally they used the *kayak*, which is small, narrow and fast and mainly used for hunting. Or they used the *umiak*, which is a larger open boat, big enough to carry whole families. Modern technology has brought new forms of transport to the Inuit. The snowmobile has replaced the dogsled and a variety of modern motorboats are used during the summer.

DOGSLEDS ON A LONG HUNT

When the sun returns in February the hunters start to think about hunting trips further away from home. These hunters are returning from a long polar bear hunt out on the ice of Melville Bay. Without their dogsleds they would be unable to travel so far out onto the ice where they can find the best hunting. The dogs are strong enough to pull heavy sleds loaded with meat back to the village.

KAYAK

This Inuk is in a *kayak* he has built for himself. It is made to fit as well as a good pair of shoes. The width of the boat at the cockpit is the length from his fingertips to his elbow plus the width of three fingers, and the length is also in proportion to his height. It is made of a wooden frame covered in sealskin or canvas.

UMIAK

An *umiak* is an open, flat-bottomed boat made by stretching walrus hide over a wooden frame. It was a craft well suited to hunting in the ice floes because it was light enough to be pulled up onto the ice if needed. It was propelled by oars and sails and had a capacity to carry a lot of people. Today *umiaks* are only used in northern Alaska and Siberia where the Inuit still use them to hunt bowhead whales and walrus during the summer months.

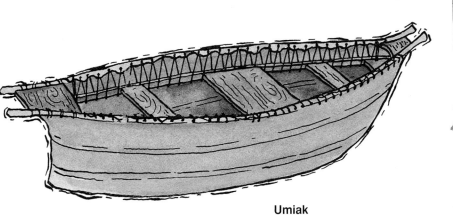

Umiak

SNOWSCOOTER

In many Canadian villages the snowscooter has replaced the dogsled as the main form of winter transport. It enables a hunter to cover long distances quickly. This has led to the overhunting of areas close to the villages and now the Inuit have to travel further to hunt. In the early days snowscooters were often unreliable and some people used to call them 'ride out and walk homes'. A dog team breeds its own replacements and eats meat while a snowscooter needs expensive fuel.

TRAVEL RESTRICTIONS

Some 25 years ago the Inuhuit saw the bad effect that snowscooters had on hunting in other parts of the Arctic. They decided that to preserve the wildlife and their culture, snowscooters would only be allowed for recreational use and not for hunting. There are also certain fjords where narwhals are known to gather and these have been made into motorboat-free zones. These restrictions on the type of transportation has meant that in Greenland the wildlife has not been overhunted as in other parts of the Arctic.

· H O W · HAVE · WE AFFECTED THE · LIVES · O F · T H E · · I N U I T ? ·

Most of us live far away from the Arctic, but the actions and decisions that take place in our countries have seriously affected the lives of the Inuit. Pollution from our heavy industries has been carried north by the wind and ocean currents, poisoning some of their traditional hunting grounds. The decision to ban the trade in sealskins by Europe and the USA has ruined the prosperity of many Inuit settlements, although the Inuit were not involved in clubbing seal pups. Traditionally the Inuit took enough furs for their personal clothing until white people encouraged them to hunt for furs to trade, but now we are telling them this is wrong. Life in settlements is expensive, and the Inuit have to find ways to earn money or rely on welfare payments.

HARP SEALS

In 1964, the 'Save the Seal' campaign was started because the public was unhappy about the killing of baby harp seals. This was being done by people who live in Canada but south of the Arctic. The Inuit do kill seals but only the young adults and not the white-coated babies. However, they suddenly found that because Europe and the USA wanted to ban sealskins, they could no longer sell theirs. They still kill seals to eat, but now they feed many of the skins to their dogs.

POISONOUS POLAR BEARS

Since the early 1970s, a great deal of work has been done on polar bears. These scientists are taking samples from a drugged bear. They can tell its age from a tooth sample, and its weight from its length and chest measurements. From blood and fat samples the scientists have been able to check the rising level of pollutants accumulating in the bear's body. If these continue to rise at the same rate, polar bears will be as poisonous as toxic waste by the year 2005.

Before the Inuit met white people their land provided everything they needed. They had clever ways of making the best of what was available. When the first traders arrived they introduced the Inuit to things they couldn't find locally. Soon their lives changed so they began to need products like bullets, coffee and tobacco and to buy these they needed money. Now they need regular work to be able to pay for the TVs and videos they want.

DISCARDED OIL DRUMS
These oil drums have been left by the American military at an old radar station in Canada. They could remain here for hundreds of years because they won't rot in the cold dry Arctic air.

SEALSKINS
The Inuit people have not stopped hunting seals because of the anti-sealing campaign. They still need the meat for food and use some of the skins for clothing. But the ban has ruined the local economy of many Inuit groups. This is because top-quality skins like these in the photograph (right) are now only worth a few pennies.

It's my world too!

INTERNATIONAL
FUND FOR
ANIMAL WELFARE

BP OIL PLANT, ALASKA
This oil production plant at Prudhoe Bay is at the start of the Alaska pipeline. The oil is pumped hundreds of kilometres to the other end of the pipeline where tankers carry it all over the world. In these hi-tech plants there are few jobs for the local Inuit and the majority of people who work the machinery come from the south. The same is true of other mining and drilling projects in the Arctic. They offer only a few unskilled jobs to local Inuit and the key jobs are held by outsiders. Because of this these projects do not offer much benefit to the Inuit community.

·WHAT·IS· HAPPENING ·TO·THE· ·INUIT?·

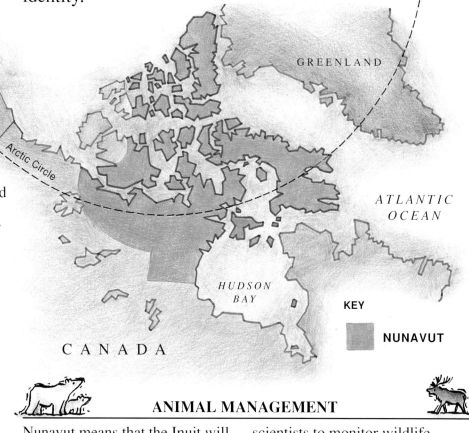

Today the Inuit have more control over their own affairs. In Greenland, Alaska and Canada they have their own television and radio stations which broadcast programmes in Inuktitut. The governments have also acknowledged the Inuit's right to their own lands. In 1979, the Inuit of Greenland received 'home rule' from Denmark, and then opted to leave the EC. In 1999, a new Inuit territory called 'Nunavut' (our land) will be created in Canada's eastern Arctic which will mean the Inuit will own 350,000 square kilometres of land, an area about the size of Norway. They will also have the opportunity to administer their own affairs, such as education, wildlife management and land use. For the Inuit it is an exciting time because they have a chance to rediscover their true identity.

NUNAVUT

Negotiations for Nunavut started in 1975, and in 1993 it was agreed to hand over control of this land to the Inuit in 1999. The next few years will be a change-over period. This allows time to make sure that enough Inuit have experience and training to administer their new territory successfully. There are plans to make Inuktitut the official language of Nunavut. This will mean that the elders who speak only that language can contribute their valuable experience and advice. They accept that it isn't going to be easy and that there are no simple solutions. No outsiders understand their lands and the people as well as the Inuit do, and after 150 years of being told how to run their lives, they are now in control.

KEY

NUNAVUT

ANIMAL MANAGEMENT

Nunavut means that the Inuit will be more involved in wildlife management. They will have a say about the methods used in hunting and the numbers of animals taken. Throughout the Arctic the Inuit people are already working with scientists to monitor wildlife populations. Everyone benefits from this, the Inuit help with samples and trapping, and in return they receive information about population figures and how hunting will affect them.

INUIT RADIO ANNOUNCER
It is hard to preserve a culture if the language is lost. In Alaska many youngsters now speak only English. Radio and TV programmes play an important part in keeping Inuktitut alive by broadcasting news of local interest to the Inuit.

INUIT 'MOUNTIE'
This Inuit Royal Canadian Mounted Policeman has a big truck and a uniform to show he has authority. As an Inuk he understands the people and the problems he is dealing with far better than a non-native would.

INUIT CHILDREN
These Inuit boys are brothers. The eldest is in the junior class at school. They have never had a better time to be educated. More of their teachers are now native Inuktitut speakers, and Nunavut promises work opportunities. There will be jobs for graduates in the administration, work for artists and crafts people in the villages and support for those who still wish to hunt.

THE FUTURE
'In the last 30 years we have gone from the stone age to the middle ages to the space age. Now the younger people are introduced to the school system at an early age. That is good, but they don't have a feel for the culture that my generation does, and there are going to be fewer and fewer young people who care. That is how cultures are lost.'

Theo Ikummaq, an Inuk.

·GLOSSARY·

ALGONQUIN Native North Americans living south of the Arctic area who speak the Algonquian language.

CARIBOU The most northerly member of the deer family which is native to Arctic regions.

CIRCUMPOLAR CONFERENCE A non-governmental organisation which represents the interests of all the native peoples of the Arctic.

EC European Community. The alliance of some European countries which formed to improve trade and economic growth.

ETHNOGRAPHERS People who study the different races of people living on Earth.

FJORD A long, narrow, rocky inlet.

ICE FLOE Floating slab of broken sea ice which can be up to 3 metres thick.

ICE EDGE Where ice attached to the land meets the open sea.

IGLULINGMIUT Inuit people from the island of Igloolik and northern Foxe Basin in Canada.

INTESTINES Part of the digestive system of a person or animal.

INUHUIT The name that the Inuit of north-west Greenland call themselves. The word means 'great and beautiful human beings' in their dialect of Inuktitut.

INUKTITUT The language spoken by Inuit people living in north-eastern Alaska, Canada and Greenland.

IVALUQ Thread made by drying thin sinews taken from the narwhal or caribou and used for sewing skins.

LANCE A wooden spear with a metal tip that was traditionally used by the Inuit for killing whales and polar bears.

MAMMAL A warm-blooded animal that feeds its young on milk.

MIGRATORY Animals that move from one place to another, such as caribou that move from winter to summer grazing grounds.

MUSK OXEN A stocky animal with huge horns and a long dark coat. It looks like a member of the cattle family but is closely related to sheep.

NARWHAL Small whale with a grey mottled skin. The males have a spiral ivory tooth up to 2 metres long, like a unicorn of the sea.

PAGAN Not Christian.

PARASITE Something that lives on something else without offering any benefit to the animal or plant it feeds off, like lice or fleas.

PERMAFROST Permanently frozen ground that may be hundreds of metres thick.

POLLUTANTS Unwanted substances that make another substance less pure.

PREY Animals hunted for food.

SHAMAN A non-Christian spiritual leader who has contact with the spirit world.

SINEWS Tough, fibre-like tissues that attach muscles to bones.

SNOW GOGGLES The Inuit's sunglasses, made from caribou antler with narrow slits to see out of. They protect the wearer from snow blindness.

SOAPSTONE A very soft stone that is easy to carve.

TABOOS A set of rituals or rules designed to keep powerful spirits happy.

TALISMAN A lucky charm with magic powers.

TREE LINE The line in the far north where trees can no longer grow because the ground is permanently frozen. North of this line, trees are small and stunted.

TUNDRA A frozen area in the Arctic, with mosses and dwarf vegetation.

TUNIQ A name believed to describe the Dorset culture people who were pushed out of the area by the ancestors of today's Inuit.

WHALERS From the 1850s, many ships from the south spent the summers in the Arctic hunting the whales for their valuable oil.

· I N D E X ·